Incredibly Disgusting Drugs™

Cocaine

Michael A. Sommers

rosen publishing's
rosen
central®

New York

Published in 2008 by The Rosen Publishing Group, Inc.
29 East 21st Street, New York, NY 10010

Copyright © 2008 by The Rosen Publishing Group, Inc.

First Edition

Library of Congress Cataloging-in-Publication Data

Sommers, Michael A.
Cocaine / Michael A. Sommers.—1st ed.
    p. cm.—(Incredibly disgusting drugs)
Includes bibliographical references and index.
ISBN-13: 978-1-4042-1379-1 (library binding)
1. Cocaine abuse. 2. Cocaine—Physiological effect. I. Title.
RC568.C6S66 2008
362.29'8—dc22

                                        2007035817

Manufactured in the United States of America

Contents

Introduction

These days, it seems as if drugs are everywhere: they're mentioned in newspapers and on entertainment Web sites, and they're talked about at parties, on college campuses, and even in schoolyards. Because kids frequently hear about them, many are curious about drugs. Some are even tempted to try them. There are numerous myths floating around about drugs. However, when you begin to learn the facts—about how drugs can affect your mind and your body, and ruin your life—you realize that the myths can be just as dangerous as the drugs themselves.

Cocaine is one of the drugs that is talked about the most. You may have heard stories about rock stars, actors, or models who use "coke." They might make it seem fashionable or glamorous. But when was the last time that rotting teeth, tremors, seizures, and heart attacks were fashionable or glamorous?

No matter how—or how many times—it is used, coke is one of the most dangerous and addictive drugs around. Indeed, it has at least as many potentially hazardous side effects as it does nicknames. Whether it is referred to as "bazooka," "beam," "Bernice," "big C," "blast," "blow," "Bolivian marching powder," "bump," "C," "candy," "Charlie coca," "flake," "rock," "snow," "snowstorm," "flake," or "toot," this deadly white powder is bad news.

Cocaine not only goes straight to your head, but it also affects essential organs such as your heart and it restricts blood flow to parts of your body. Aside from the havoc it can wreak on you physically, cocaine can also destroy your mind. It can effectively rewire your brain and mess with your nervous system. It can leave you feeling paranoid, panicked, and even psychotic. Even scarier is the fact that as you come to rely more and more on coke—and close to one-quarter of all cocaine users become abusers or addicts—you will inevitably end up sabotaging your life.

Screwing up in school, destroying relationships with friends and family members, and getting into trouble with the law are only some of the most common consequences of cocaine use. Others include going into debt, getting involved in accidents and violent situations, and plunging into a massive depression that is very hard to get out of. Death is also a possibility—either from despair so deep that it drives you to suicide or from an accidental overdose, which can kill you.

1
Kids
and Coke

n the 1970s, cocaine became popular as a recreational drug in mainstream America. However, it is one of the oldest drugs known to humanity. Made from the coca plant, which grows in South America's Andes Mountains, cocaine is the most powerful existing natural stimulant. It is also one of the most addictive because it directly affects—and alters—your brain.

In 2006, the National Institute on Drug Abuse (NIDA) completed a nationwide survey on kids and cocaine. The institute found that 3.4 percent of eighth graders, 4.8 percent of tenth graders, and 8.5 percent of twelfth graders had used cocaine at least once. In addition, a 2005 Substance Abuse and Mental Health Services Administration (SAMHSA) survey reported that 25 percent of people between the ages of twelve and seventeen said it would be easy for them to get cocaine if they wanted to. However, the real question is: Who would want it?

Above, in Machacarmarka, Bolivia, north of the capital city of La Paz, indigenous workers harvest coca leaves. Although the Bolivian government allows its people to cultivate coca leaves, according to U.S. authorities, some of Bolivia's land is allegedly used for drug producing.

Coke Is Cool?

Did you know that each year, more than 300,000 Americans—most of them teens—try cocaine for the first time? Many kids initially snort coke because they think it's cool or that it makes them more grown-up. There are a lot of other reasons kids use cocaine, but none of them are very convincing. Kids try coke because it's available, because their friends do it, because they think—wrongly—that it's not as dangerous as other drugs such as crystal meth or heroin, or because adults (particularly celebrities) use it. As reasons for taking a drug that could harm or kill you, these are pretty lame.

Use and Abuse

The most common way of taking cocaine is through the nose, which is known as snorting or sniffing. Snorting is the none-too-attractive process of inhaling cocaine powder through the nostrils, where it is absorbed into the bloodstream via the nasal tissues. Usually this is done using a tightly rolled-up piece of paper or a plastic straw—the sharing of which can lead to the passing on of contagious blood diseases such as hepatitis C.

However, there are other ways of using cocaine. Injecting cocaine into your veins with a needle—a painful practice known as mainlining—releases the drug directly into the bloodstream and heightens the intensity of its effects. In fact, the effects are so intense that they can cause users to start vomiting uncontrollably. Meanwhile "smoking" coke involves breathing in, or inhaling, the fumes of heated cocaine. The smoke then travels into the lungs and is absorbed into the bloodstream, providing an immediate rush. Some users smoke cocaine by mixing it with marijuana in a cigarette. Others do coke orally, rubbing the powder directly onto their gums. Because doing this numbs the gums and teeth, coke hits taken this way are known as "numbies," "gummies," or "cocoa puffs." Another oral method of taking coke is to wrap up some powder in rolling paper and swallow it, which is known as a "snowbomb."

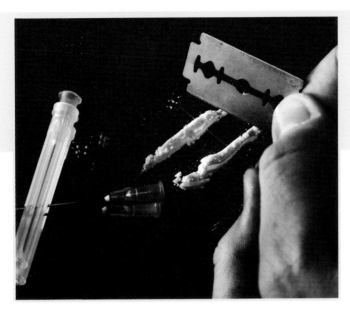

A cocaine user creates "lines" of coke with a razor blade. The drug can then be snorted or injected by needle directly into the blood.

Cocaine abuse can range from occasional to repeated and compulsive use (addiction). However, it doesn't matter how, or how often, it is used—there is no safe way to use cocaine. There is always the risk that the body will absorb toxic, or poisonous, amounts of the drug. The result can be heart or brain seizures so severe that they could lead to sudden death.

So Exciting?

Once they have tried cocaine, some kids find they like the initial sensation of excited pleasure that they experience when they use it. And it's true that cocaine, which goes straight to the brain and affects the way the nervous system operates, will produce a short-lived "high" and a "rush" of energy (accompanied by a racing heartbeat and high blood pressure

Origins of Coke

In Peru and Bolivia, indigenous peoples who live high in the Andes Mountains have used the leaves of the coca plant for centuries. When chewed, the leaves act as a very mild stimulant, which helps fight the weariness that comes with working at high altitudes where the air is thinner.

Around 500 pounds (227 kilograms) of coca leaves, which are worth about $500, are needed to manufacture a pound (less than half a kilogram) of cocaine. To produce cocaine, coca leaves are placed in a pit, and then kerosene and acid are added. This poisonous mixture is then crushed and stomped upon (often by poor, underage workers in Peru, Bolivia, and Colombia) until it becomes a thick liquid. The liquid is left in the sun so it forms a paste. When dried, the paste is crumbled into a powder known as cocaine hydrochloride, or pure cocaine.

Half of all the cocaine produced in the world is shipped illegally from South America to the United States. Then the pure cocaine is cut, or mixed, five or six times with other substances. This makes the drug weaker; only around 20 percent of the cocaine that users snort, smoke, or mainline is really coke. The rest could be anything from cornstarch to more dangerous substances like local anesthetics.

that can lead to a heart attack). However, after this brief sensation of well-being passes, one will quickly return to normal. Only "normal" won't feel so good anymore after the artificial roller-coaster ride.

Instead, people who come "down" from a coke binge tend to feel exactly that: down. So, they will start snorting more coke in an attempt to get that high again. Before they know it, they are hooked. If you think it takes years and years to become a cocaine addict, think again. Coke is considered one of the most dangerously addictive of all drugs. Even if you use it only once, it alters your brain chemistry and leaves you craving more and more. In fact, a person can become addicted to coke after just one session.

The Great Escape

Aside from peer pressure, curiosity, or the desire to take a risk or feel excited, kids also turn to coke because they see it as an escape from the problems in their lives. They might feel insecure, unpopular, or unhappy at school. They may be dealing with stress or family problems at home. They may even have parents or older brothers or sisters who use and abuse cocaine and other drugs. Therefore, they think that taking drugs is a way of dealing with troubles—even if it just creates more.

No matter how difficult a time you may be going through, believing that a drug will solve the problem is the worst expectation you can have. In the short run, coke might give you a boost of energy, a high, or a sensation of feeling as invincible as Superman or Wonder Woman. However, these very temporary sensations are all tricks caused by a dangerous chemical

Drugs may seem like a way to escape problems or unhappiness. However, although the teenage years can be difficult, using drugs won't make life any easier.

affecting your brain. One thing that you can be sure about with cocaine is that it won't solve any of your problems. It will create more. You might go bankrupt paying for your drug habit, ruin your physical and mental health, and destroy relationships with friends and family members. Instead of providing a welcome escape, cocaine will make your life a living nightmare.

The $\overset{2}{\text{Inside Story:}}$
How Cocaine Affects the Body

Cocaine is known as a party drug because some people think it makes a party more fun. Obviously, they don't think much of the people who they hang out with—or themselves—if they depend on a drug to have a good time. However, coke's party-enhancing reputation has given it a glamorous edge that it really doesn't deserve. If you think that "beautiful people" such as movie stars and models do coke and look just great, then the inside reality offers a whole other story.

If You Only Had a Brain . . .

Cocaine goes straight to your head, literally, and messes with your brain's nerve cells, throwing your body and mind out of whack. Snorting coke can lead you to start behaving in strange and even violent ways.

The truth is, there is no telling how you might react or what you might end up doing—especially when you consider that most cocaine is not pure but is mixed with

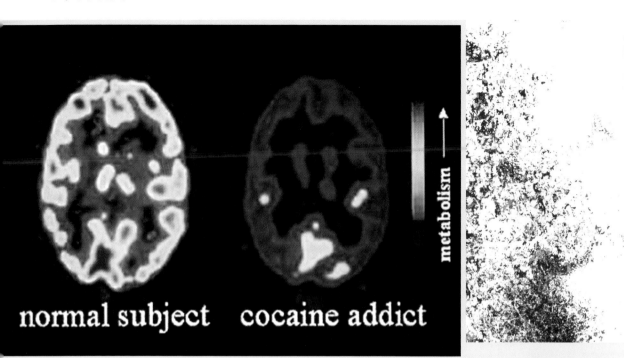

normal subject   cocaine addict

These PET (positron-emission tomography) scans show how cocaine can alter the brain. The metabolism of a nonuser's brain *(left)* is much higher than that of a cocaine addict's brain *(right)*.

other substances ranging from cornstarch and sugar to unknown and often dangerous chemicals. After all, it's not as if cocaine is sold in packages that list the ingredients. Even drug dealers don't always know what is in the stuff that they sell. Ultimately, the only thing that is certain is that you don't know what you are putting in your body and how it is going to affect you. What has been proven, however, is that using coke can result in brain seizures and strokes.

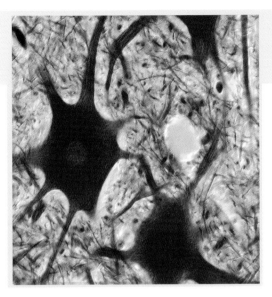

This microscopic image shows normal neurons, or nerve cells of the brain, interacting with one another.

Dirty Tricks

Stimulants such as cocaine transform the way that your brain works. This is because they affect how your nerve cells communicate with each other. Nerve cells, known as neurons, send messages to each other by releasing special chemicals called neurotransmitters. There are different types of neurotransmitters, but the one that is most affected by cocaine is dopamine.

Whenever you do something that gives you pleasure—whether it's eating a bag of potato chips, scoring a winning goal, or kissing someone you have a crush on—dopamine is released into your brain, filling you with a sensation of intense happiness. When people use cocaine and other stimulants, it causes dopamine to build up in the brain and this, in turn, makes users feel a high. However, the high isn't natural. It is caused by stimulants that are tricking the brain, and the trick is a really dirty one because the sad fact is that the more you use cocaine, the

The "Glamorous" Drug?

A lot of people think cocaine is glamorous because of the number of celebrities whose drug use is talked about in tabloids and on Web sites. Recently, for example, all eyes were on actress Lindsay Lohan, who was arrested in July 2007 on counts of drunk driving and cocaine possession.

On the surface, Lohan may seem to have everything going for her. But according to statements made by her friends, the Hollywood star's cocaine use means that she's out of control a lot of the time. Her arrest happened shortly after she left a drug and alcohol rehabilitation clinic. The fact that she apparently was not cured is proof of how hard it is to kick a cocaine habit. In the meantime, this talented young actress is facing a possible jail sentence. Her increasingly unstable reputation threatens to ruin a very promising acting career.

more confused your brain will become. Eventually, the way your brain functions can be permanently altered.

Over time, the brain's dopamine receptors will actually decrease. This means that cocaine users will lose the ability to naturally feel any pleasure at all. This is how people become addicts. Frustrated at no longer being able to feel happiness without chemicals, they take more and more cocaine in order to continue tricking the brain into producing more dopamine. Of course, since the dopamine receptors have been dulled, users will have to take immense amounts of coke just to feel the slightest high. This is why addicts eventually become so hooked—and so miserable.

Serious Addiction

It is possible to become addicted to cocaine very quickly. Once you are hooked, the addiction can be extremely difficult to break. Studies carried out on laboratory animals such as monkeys found that if given a choice between cocaine, and food and water, they always chose cocaine. In fact, many would rather have starved than give up coke. Moreover, the animals also demonstrated that they were willing to physically exhaust themselves (pressing a bar more than ten thousand times) in order to receive a single injection of cocaine. They took cocaine even though they knew that doing so would result in punishment. In fact, the animals studied had to have cocaine taken away from them, or else they would have overdosed and died.

Sadly, human cocaine addicts, like the lab animals, will stop at nothing to score the drug. They don't care if they get kicked out of school or lose their jobs, or if they drive away their loved ones and spend all the money they have. Often, addicts sell off all their possessions and resort to theft in order to get their hands on cocaine. According to a study published by CocaineAddiction.com, cocaine is the most addictive and frequently abused drug in the United States, second only to heroin. In 2002, more than 25 percent of American cocaine users were considered to be abusers or addicts of the drug.

Mind Games

Coke's effects appear almost immediately after it is used and are gone within a short amount of time. After the initial rush, which lasts from ten to thirty minutes, you can expect your mind to play tricks on you. Aside from restlessness, irritability, confusion, and anxiety, you may experience things around you in a heightened—and not always pleasant—way.

The more you use cocaine, the worse the mind games will become. This is because the more coke you use, the more your mind will build up a tolerance to the highs that the drug produces. This means that in order to experience the same effects, you will have to take greater amounts of cocaine. It also means that the side effects will get worse, causing you to suffer from uncontrollable mood swings. Hallucinations—seeing and hearing things that aren't really present—are common. In fact, some regular users develop a hallucination in which they are sure that they can feel insects known as "coke bugs" crawling all over their skin. Another common sensation is paranoia, in which you feel certain that everybody is out to get you. There is even the chance of developing full-blown paranoid psychosis, in which you will completely lose touch with reality.

"Cocaine frenzy" is the term used to describe users who begin displaying violent and psychotic behavior after they take cocaine. Like small animals or birds when trapped in a cage, these users can become so panicky and

PALM SPRINGS

POLICE DEPARTMENT

MUGSHOT PROFILE

NAME:	DOWNEY	ROBERT	J
AKA:			
CASE NUMBER:	00-3300043		
CII:	A11290504		
MNI#:			
BOOKING #:	00-004687		
PHOTO#:	40007068		
PHOTO DATE/TIME:	11 / 26 / 00 00 :55		
DATE OF BIRTH:			
AGE AT ARREST:	35		
SOCIAL SECURITY #:			
DL STATE:	CALIFORNIA		
DL NUMBER:			
ADDRESS:		BLV -	
CITY:	LOS A		
STATE:	CALIFORNIA		

PHYSICAL DESCRIPTION

SEX:	MALE
RACE:	WHITE
HEIGHT:	5'09"
WEIGHT:	165

Film and television actor Robert Downey Jr. battled drug addiction for years. The mug shot (above) was taken following a 2000 arrest for cocaine possession.

upset that they can die of shock. They can also be extremely brutal and destructive. They may get into fights, destroy property, and—because they lose all sense of limits—pull stupid stunts (such as driving too fast or jumping out of a window) that can injure or kill them and others.

One victim of cocaine frenzy, cited on Dr. Joseph C. Rupp's "Drugs and Death" Web site, was a man who first attracted attention when he ran from a house into the street shouting crazily. Witnesses were shocked to see that the man (who had actually gone on a cocaine binge) had gouged out one of his eyes with his fingers and was stabbing himself with a kitchen knife. An ambulance arrived to take him to a hospital. In the emergency room, he grabbed a syringe full of his own blood and threatened to attack the nurses and doctors who were trying to save him. A police officer on the scene repeatedly ordered him to drop the syringe. When he wouldn't obey, the officer was forced to shoot the man in self-defense. Although he didn't die, he did lose his gouged-out eye.

Blood Simple

When cocaine enters the body, it causes blood vessels to become narrower, or constricted, limiting the flow of blood. This forces the heart to work harder pumping blood through the body. It also increases blood pressure. If you have ever tried fitting into a pair of jeans that are three sizes too small, then you may have some idea of the difficulty that the heart has in pumping blood through narrowed vessels. Having constricted blood vessels also means that blood has a harder time reaching other parts of the body. If blood flow is reduced over a long period of time, organ tissue can die. When this happens, gangrene, a serious condition that is the result of dead tissue, sets in. Limbs with gangrene begin to smell. They shrivel up and turn black or blue. Often, the only way to deal with gangrene—and to prevent it from spreading—is by performing surgery or amputating the dead body part.

One terrible example of the consequences of narrowed blood vessels is bowel gangrene. This condition is as bad as it sounds. Narrowed vessels cutting off blood flow to the bowel can cause tissue from the intestinal wall to die. This causes severe diarrhea, stomach pains, and fever. Furthermore, the subsequent swelling and infection of the abdomen, if not quickly treated, can result in death.

Heart of the Matter

With the increased work it takes to pump blood through constricted vessels, the heart has to beat faster. It may beat so fast that it temporarily loses its natural rhythm. This is called fibrillation, and it can be life threatening because it results in the suspension of blood flow throughout your body. Cocaine may also cause the blood vessels in the heart to constrict so much that blood flow to this essential organ is completely cut off. Without blood, the heart can't keep beating. Without a heartbeat, it is impossible to live.

The photo at right of leg and foot gangrene shows a possible side effect of cocaine use. Cocaine can cause blood vessels to constrict, leading to the death of cell tissue.

Cocaine use can trigger many other heart problems as well. A variety of unpleasant symptoms range from chest pains, nausea, dizziness, and convulsions to blurred vision, muscle spasms, tremors, and mild-to-severe breathing problems. Meanwhile, people who use coke are seven times more likely than nonusers to have a heart attack over the course of their lives. Within the hour that cocaine is first taken, chances of having a heart attack increase by twenty-four times!

The
Outside Story:
Cocaine's Effects
on Appearance

Coke can wreak havoc on your insides, causing irreparable damage to your organs and even resulting in death. However, the drug can also cause a great deal of harm to your outsides.

The Nose Knows

One of the most common ways of using cocaine is inhaling the powder up your nose. Aside from the financial price that snorters pay for the drug, their actual nostrils pay a price as well.

Forget about smelling flowers, perfume, or freshly baked brownies; regularly snorting cocaine can lead to loss of sense of smell. You should also make sure you start carrying around a big hanky, since nosebleeds are frequent among those who snort cocaine. Aside from eventually destroying the entire lining of your nose, you can expect lots of serious nasal infections. This will lead to having a constantly swollen, red, and runny nose.

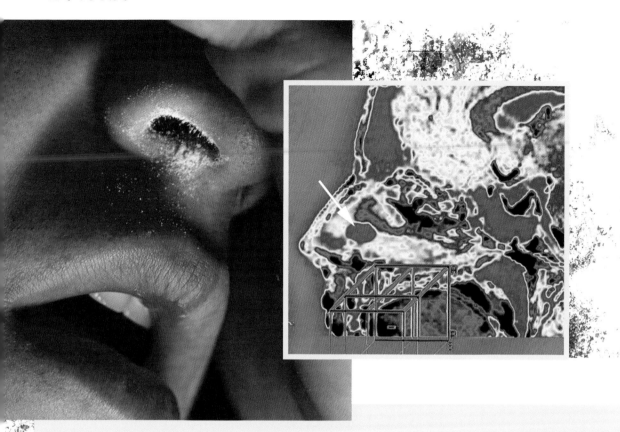

The photograph at left shows cocaine powder remaining around a man's nostril after he has snorted the drug. The MRI (magnetic resonance image) in the inset shows a perforation, or hole, in a nasal septum resulting from cocaine use.

Mouthing Off

Ingesting coke through either the nose or the mouth can lead to problems swallowing and a hoarse, raspy voice. In addition, people who take cocaine orally—usually by rubbing the powder along their gums—can end up with rotten teeth.

A Tragic Tale

Harold Hunter is only one of the latest in a long line of celebrities who died too young because they took a fatal overdose of cocaine. Hunter's outsized personality and skateboarding talent led him to modeling and movie roles, celebrity friendships, and fame as a downtown, native New Yorker who was part of the underground scene. However, it also led him to a cocaine habit. Despite roles on TV shows and in films such as *Kids* (1995); appearing in ads for the likes of designer Tommy Hilfiger; and tours with Zoo York, a famous New York skateboarding team, Hunter developed a coke addiction. This meant that he never had a penny to his name. When Hunter died of a heart attack as a result of a massive cocaine overdose in February 2006, his celebrity pals had to pitch in to pay for his funeral and burial. Hunter was only thirty-one years old.

The Skeletal Look

Because cocaine messes with your brain's impulses, one of the many side effects is a loss of appetite. (This is one of the reasons that cocaine is popular with actors and models.) Sure, lots of people would like to be thinner, but serious coke addicts develop a look that is anything but

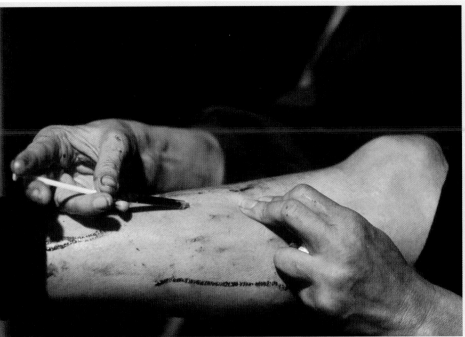

Above, a user injects a speedball—a dangerous mixture of cocaine and heroin—into his leg. Besides terrible scarring, injecting drugs can lead to serious infections.

healthy. Instead, they look downright skeletal due to malnourishment and lack of appetite.

On Your Marks

It is one thing to decorate your body with tattoos and piercings. It is quite another to walk around sporting bruises and puncture marks, known as tracks. People who inject cocaine directly into their veins with a needle don't look so good. Because coke constricts the blood vessels in the skin, needle sites are often sickly pale and covered with large, ugly scabs. Even worse is the fact that constricted blood vessels reduce blood flow to different tissues, including the skin. Over a period of time, dead skin can result in the formation of horrible scars.

Moreover, a lot of things can go wrong when you try to inject drugs. Some coke users have been known to aim for a vein in the arm but end up injecting coke into an artery by mistake. As a result, the artery can constrict, cutting off blood to the arm and hand. In some cases, this kills tissue so quickly that doctors have no choice other than to amputate the drug users' "dead" fingers and hands.

Although wearing long sleeves and long pants might hide the unsightly track marks, it doesn't stop the risk of allergic reaction. Reactions can be either to the drug itself or to unknown additives in the powder, which can make you sick and even kill you. Not to mention that with needle use, there is always the risk of infecting yourself with foreign bacteria or viruses such as HIV (human immunodeficiency virus), the virus that causes AIDS (acquired immunodeficiency syndrome).

4
Complications

On its own, cocaine is bad enough. After all, you can never know exactly what has been mixed with the white powder when you're putting it into your body. But when you take coke together with other substances, the effects can be more hazardous and deadly.

Crack

The most dangerous and addictive form of cocaine is called crack cocaine. Instead of a powder, it looks like a chip or a rock. Crack is a very potent form of cocaine that can be smoked. It is made by melting down cocaine powder, mixing it with baking soda, and cooking it to form a paste. After hardening into a rock, it can be heated. Its fumes can be inhaled into the lungs, giving the user an immediate—but fleeting—high. Crack got its name from the crackling sound that it makes when it is smoked.

Crack cocaine is sold in small chunks that resemble rocks. Each rock contains a tiny amount of water. Heating the drug causes this water to boil and make a cracking sound.

Crack is much cheaper than cocaine, and it can be bought in small quantities. This makes it a major temptation for adolescents and people who can't afford cocaine. Crack is extremely addictive: once people start smoking it, they crave more and more of it. And since crack's effects are intense but fleeting (lasting only five to fifteen minutes), users want more of the drug almost immediately. In fact, many crack houses, where users buy and smoke crack, depend on these cravings. They offer users a place to smoke and an endless supply of small bags for purchase.

Meanwhile, because crack is so addictive, users are prepared to do anything—steal, lie, and even kill—in order to get it. For this reason, the United States has tough laws against selling and possessing crack. These laws are harsher than those concerning all other illegal substances because crack is in a class of danger by itself.

A man smokes crack in an apartment in the New York City neighborhood of Washington Heights. Cocaine and crack have transformed many urban neighborhoods into war zones ruled by drug dealers and users (as Washington Heights was in the 1990s).

Deadly Duos

Some street dealers mix cocaine with other drugs such as procaine (a synthetic local anesthetic widely known under the trade name Novocain) or with other stimulants, like amphetamines. Some users combine cocaine or crack with heroin in a "speedball." Users may think that two drugs are better than one. In reality, such drug cocktails are recipes for trouble because the possible dangers are multiplied.

Chris Rock, David Spade, and Chris Farley *(left to right)* all starred on *Saturday Night Live* in the early to mid-1990s. Farley died in 1997 from a cocaine overdose.

In the 1980s and 1990s, several famous actors suffered tragic deaths due to speedballing. John Belushi, an actor and comedian, became famous through the television show *Saturday Night Live*. He was only thirty-three years old when he died of an accidental overdose. Chris Farley was another promising comedian who began his career on *Saturday Night Live* (at the same time as the actor/ comedian Chris Rock). Ironically, Farley's idol was Belushi. Tragically, Farley died just like his hero—from an overdose at the age of thirty-three. Another shocking death was that of twenty-three-year-old actor River Phoenix in 1993. He was the older brother of Joaquin Phoenix, who starred as Johnny Cash in the Oscar-winning film *Walk the Line*. At the time of his death from an overdose at a Los Angeles nightclub, River Phoenix had been nominated for an Oscar and a Golden Globe. Many considered him the most talented actor of his generation.

People who abuse both cocaine and alcohol compound the danger each drug poses. When combined with alcohol, cocaine can become even more toxic, causing particular harm to the liver. NIDA-funded researchers have found that when the human liver is exposed to both cocaine and alcohol, it manufactures a third substance called cocaethylene. Cocaethylene intensifies cocaine's effects, possibly increasing the risk of sudden death. Scarily, since coke is a "club drug," often taken at night in a party atmosphere, users frequently take it while drinking large amounts of alcohol.

It's a Crime

In North America, buying, selling, possessing, and using cocaine and crack—no matter how small the amount—is against the law. Just carrying around a tiny bit in your pocket is a crime, and it is enough to put you in prison. U.S. laws are particularly tough on those in possession of crack. Currently, first-time offenders can spend at least five years behind bars for possessing five grams (0.18 ounces) of crack, which is the weight of five paper clips. Possession of cocaine can result in up to seven years in prison. Selling, carrying, or even delivering it can lead to a lifetime in jail.

Even if you don't spend years behind bars, having a drug record will follow you for the rest of your life. It will prevent you from getting into schools where you want to study and it will diminish job possibilities. In terms of travel, some countries won't provide a visa to people who have a drug record.

Overdose and Death

Using coke is no joke. It can be fatal, even if you're just trying it. In rare instances, sudden death can occur the very first time you take the drug,

A suspect is arrested on a felony charge in August 2006, after police found three ounces of pure crack hidden in his car.

or shortly after. You don't even have to overdose. Most cocaine-related deaths are the result of cardiac arrest or seizures caused by the drug, which make it impossible for you to breathe.

Even the healthiest—and happiest—people can die this way. In 1986, a twenty-three-year-old college basketball star named Len Bias was on top of the world after just having been drafted to play professional ball with the Boston Celtics. Tragically, only forty-eight hours after he signed

Len Bias expresses his happiness at being selected second overall in the 1986 NBA draft. Two days later, he was dead from a cocaine overdose.

the contract, Bias—who was already being compared with basketball superstar Michael Jordan—had a heart seizure in his college dorm after celebrating with his teammates. The heart attack was brought on by cocaine use. In 2002, Hollywood director Ted Demme died of a heart attack at age thirty-eight, while playing a game of basketball. Cocaine was found in his system. Also in 2002, John Entwistle, composer and bass guitar player for the legendary British rock band the Who, died in a Las Vegas hotel room after overdosing on cocaine. His death occurred the night before the Who were scheduled to kick off a nationwide tour. All of these talented people seemed to have everything going for them. Cocaine use not only ended their promising careers, but their lives as well.

People who use coke over long periods risk death. As time goes by, some users increase the amount of coke they take in order to prolong the high that becomes harder and harder to achieve. Meanwhile, when the effects of the coke wear off, the resulting "down" feels worse and worse.

In fact, the terrible depression experienced can be so extreme that it has been known to drive some addicts to commit suicide.

In order to fight these feelings of depression, users will do anything to get their hands on more cocaine. They might also start to binge, which means they use higher doses of coke. An overdose can put you in a coma. Even worse, as with John Belushi, Chris Farley, River Phoenix, and Len Bias, an overdose can kill you.

While most people's tolerance to coke increases over time, driving them to use more and more of the drug, some users' bodies can actually become more sensitive to the drug's effects. This explains why some die from taking low doses of cocaine.

Staying Clear and Clean

It's not necessarily easy to "just say no" to drugs. Cocaine, in particular, is widely available. Sadly, it is also widely accepted among many adults. Since it is talked about a lot, people let down their guard and think that cocaine is not so dangerous. But there is no way of knowing how cocaine will affect *you*. The only things you can be sure of are the facts, and the facts show that cocaine is highly addictive and can harm you and even cause you to die.

Getting Help

If you or someone you know has a problem with cocaine or crack, there are many places you can go for information and help. Aside from talking to a school guidance counselor or health-care professional, get in touch with

Signs of Addiction

How can you tell if you or someone you know may have a cocaine or crack addiction? According to the NIDA, health-care professionals who screen for drug use often ask questions such as the following to detect substance abuse in their adolescent patients:

- Have you ever ridden in a car driven by someone (including yourself) who had been using alcohol or drugs?
- Do you ever use alcohol or drugs to relax, feel better about yourself, or fit in?
- Do you ever use alcohol or drugs when you are alone?
- Do you ever forget things you did while using alcohol or drugs?
- Do your family or friends ever tell you to cut down on your drinking or drug use?
- Have you ever gotten into trouble while you were using alcohol or drugs?

Narcotics Anonymous (NA) or Cocaine Anonymous (CA), organizations that specialize in dealing with cocaine addiction. With local chapters all over the United States and Canada, they can help you and your loved ones get the help needed to overcome this dangerous addiction and stay clean, healthy, and happy.

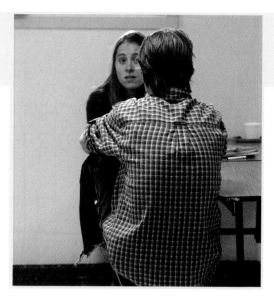

Learning to live without drugs is a long and difficult process. Counseling is an essential part of ongoing treatment.

Getting over a cocaine or crack addiction is not easy. Coke and crack are two of the most powerfully psychologically addictive substances that are out there. For this reason, professional treatment is often necessary to help addicts kick the habit and stay clean. Treatment usually involves therapy along with counseling where users learn how to adapt to and maintain a drug-free lifestyle.

Addicts have to learn how to deal with their problems without depending on drugs. They also have to stay away from tempting situations that could cause them to start using cocaine again. In most cases, one-on-one therapy with an addiction counselor is combined with peer support groups such as NA and CA. Treatment typically isn't a question of weeks or months, but of years. In the meantime, medical researchers in both Canada and the United States are hard at work trying to discover medications that would block the severe craving for cocaine experienced by addicts, which can prevent them from recovering.

Ultimately, however, the only surefire way of fighting addiction is by not becoming a user in the first place. Indeed, since cocaine is such an addictive drug to begin with, the smartest and kindest thing you can do for yourself when someone offers you cocaine is to say, "No thanks."

Glossary

amphetamines Stimulant drugs that have effects similar to those of cocaine.

anesthetic An agent that causes insensitivity to pain; it is often used prior to surgery and other medical procedures.

artery Major blood vessel that transports blood from the heart to other body parts.

binge A period or spree of excessive alcohol or drug use.

compound *(noun)* Composed of two or more parts, elements, or ingredients; *(verb)* to make worse.

constrict To narrow.

crack Slang term for a highly addictive form of cocaine that is smoked.

crystal meth Short for crystal methamphetamine, a highly powerful and addictive man-made stimulant that is smoked or injected.

dopamine A type of neurotransmitter (brain chemical) that regulates emotions, particularly sensations of pleasure.

gangrene A serious condition brought on by the death of organ tissue due to a lack of blood circulation.

fibrillation A condition in which the heart beats so fast that it loses its natural rhythm.

hepatitis C A disease that causes inflammation of the liver.

heroin A highly addictive drug made from morphine that gives users a high.

HIV (human immunodeficiency virus) A virus that attacks the immune system and causes AIDS (acquired immunodeficiency syndrome).

indigenous Native, or originating in and typical of a region or country.

kerosene A type of oil used as fuel for cooking and heating; it is made from distilled petroleum.

mainline To inject cocaine directly into one's veins.

marijuana The dried leaves of the hemp plant; they have relaxing and hallucinogenic properties when smoked. Marijuana is considered an illegal drug.

neuron Nerve cell.

neurotransmitters Special chemicals that "take messages" from one neuron to another.

overdose To take an excessive dose of a drug.

speedball A dangerous mixture of cocaine and heroin.

stimulant A type of drug that elevates mood, increases feelings of well-being, and increases energy.

tolerance A condition in which higher doses of a drug are required to produce the same effect that occurred during initial use.

For More Information

Canadian Centre on Substance Abuse

75 Albert Street, Suite 300

Ottawa, ON K1P 5E7

Canada

(613) 235-4048

Web site: http://www.ccsa.ca/ccsa

This government organization conducts research and develops programs to prevent and reduce social problems caused by drug and alcohol use throughout Canada.

Canadian Health Network

Public Health Agency of Canada

Jeanne Mance Building, 10th Floor

Tunney's Pasture, A.L. 1910B

Ottawa, ON K1A 0K9

Canada

Web site: http://www.canadian-health-network.ca

Canada's national health network has links to more than eight hundred resources throughout the country, including school, work, and community programs that can help identify, prevent, and deal with diseases and addictions.

Cocaine Anonymous World Services

3740 Overland Avenue, Suite C

Los Angeles, CA 90034

(310) 559-5833

Web site: http://www.ca.org
This organization uses a twelve-step program to help people recover from cocaine abuse.

Community Anti-Drug Coalitions of America (CADCA)

625 Slaters Lane, Suite 300

Alexandria, VA 22314

(800) 54-CADCA (542-2322)

Web site: http://cadca.org
CADCA brings together more than five thousand community groups across the United States to help coordinate and develop antidrug programs.

Narcotics Anonymous World Services, Inc.

P.O. Box 9999

Van Nuys, CA 91409

(818) 773-9999

Web site: http://www.na.org
This world service office of Narcotics Anonymous (NA) can help you find general information about the organization, helpful literature, and how to locate and contact local NA services.

National Drug Intelligence Center

319 Washington Street, 5th Floor

Johnstown, PA 15901-1622

(814) 532-4601

Web site: http://www.usdoj.gov/ndic/index.htm
This branch of the U.S. Department of Justice is committed to providing intelligence about illegal drug activities.

National Institute on Drug Abuse (NIDA)

National Institutes of Health

6001 Executive Boulevard, Room 5213

Bethesda, MD 20892-9561

(301) 443-1124

Web site: http://www.nida.nih.gov
NIDA focuses on scientific research to find out more about the effects of drugs and drug abuse in order to improve prevention and treatment and combat addiction.

Office of National Drug Control Policy

Drug Policy Information Clearinghouse

P.O. Box 6000

Rockville, MD 20849-6000

(800) 666–3332

Web site: http://www.whitehousedrugpolicy.gov
The goals of this White House drug program are to reduce the illegal use, manufacture, and selling of drugs, as well as drug-related crime and health problems.

Substance Abuse and Mental Health Services Administration (SAMHSA)

1 Choke Cherry Road

Rockville, MD 20857

(800) 273-8255

Web site: http://www.samhsa.gov
Part of the U.S. Department of Health and Human Services, SAMHSA increases awareness about substance abuse and develops programs for prevention and treatment of addiction.

Web Sites

Due to the changing nature of Internet links, Rosen Publishing has developed an online list of Web sites related to the subject of this book. This site is updated regularly. Please use this link to access the list:

http://www.rosenlinks.com/idd/coca

For Further Reading

Aretha, David. *Cocaine and Crack* (Drugs). Berkeley
    Heights, NJ: Enslow Publishers, 2005.

Bayer, Linda, Ph.D. *Crack & Cocaine* (Junior Drug Awareness).
    New York, NY: Chelsea House Publications, 2000.

Carlson-Berne, Emma, ed. *Cocaine* (The History of Drugs).
    Detroit, MI: Greenhaven Press, 2005.

Connolly, Sean. *Cocaine* (Straight Talking). North Mankato, MN:
    Smart Apple Media, 2006.

Crist, James J., Ph.D. *When Someone You Love Abuses
    Alcohol or Drugs: A Guide for Kids*. Gretna, LA: Wellness
    Institute, 2003.

Hyde, Margaret O., and John F. Setaro, M.D. *Drugs 101: An
    Overview for Teens*. Minneapolis, MN: Twenty-First Century
    Books, 2003.

Landau, Elaine *Cocaine*. New York, NY: Franklin Watts, 2003.

Lennard-Brown, Sarah. *Cocaine* (Health Issues). Chicago, IL:
    Raintree, 2004.

LeVert, Suzanne. *The Facts About Cocaine*. Tarrytown, NY:
    Benchmark Books, 2006.

Marshall, Shelly. *Young, Sober, and Free: Experience, Strength,
    and Hope for Young Adults*. 2nd ed. Center City, MN:
    Hazelden, 2003.

Bibliography

Cocaine Addiction.com. Retrieved July 2007 (http://www.cocaineaddiction.com).

National Clearinghouse for Drug and Alcohol Information. "Tips for Teens: The Truth About Cocaine." Retrieved July 2007 (http://ncadi.samhsa.gov/govpubs/phd640).

National Institute on Drug Abuse. "NIDA Info Facts: Crack and Cocaine." Retrieved July 2007 (http://www.nida.nih.gov/infofacts/cocaine.html).

NIDA for Teens. "The Science Behind Drug Abuse." Retrieved July 2007 (http://teens.drugabuse.gov).

Office of National Drug Control Policy. "Drug Facts: Cocaine." Retrieved July 2007 (http://www.whitehousedrugpolicy.gov/drugfact/cocaine/index.html).

Rupp, Joseph C., M.D., Ph.D. "Cocaine." Drugs and Death: Profiles of Illegal Drug Abuse. Retrieved July 2007 (http://deep6inc.com/previewcoc04.html).

Ryzik, Melena. "Cocaine: Hidden in Plain Sight." NYTimes.com. June 10, 2007. Retrieved July 2007 (http://www.nytimes.com/2007/06/10/fashion/10cocaine.html?_r=1&oref=slogin&pagewanted=all).

Teen Drug Abuse. "Cocaine Use Among Teens." Retrieved July 2007 (http://www.teendrugabuse.us/teen_cocaine_use.html).

Index

About the Author

Michael A. Sommers was born in Texas and raised in Canada. After earning a bachelor's degree in English literature at McGill University, in Montreal, Canada, he went on to complete a master's degree in history and civilizations from the Ecole des Hautes Etudes en Sciences Sociales, in Paris, France. For the last fifteen years, Sommers has worked as a writer and photographer. He has previously written other titles in Rosen's Incredibly Disgusting Drugs series, including *Tobacco and Your Mouth* and *Steroids and Your Muscles*.

Photo Credits

Cover, p. 1 © www.istockphoto.com/stockphoto4u; pp. 3, 10, 16, 25, 29, 36, 39, 41, 45, 46, 47 Courtesy of the U.S. Drug Enforcement Administration; p. 7 © AFP/Getty Images; pp. 9, 12 Shutterstock.com; p. 14 © Science VU/Visuals Unlimited; p. 15 © Biophoto Associates/Photo Researchers, Inc.; pp. 19, 33, 34 © Getty Images; p. 21 © M. English, MD/Custom Medical Stock Photo; p. 24 © Oscar Burriel/Photo Researchers, Inc.; p. 24 (inset) © Cavalleni/Custom Medical Stock Photo; p. 26 © A. Ramey/Photo Edit; p. 30 © AP Images; p. 31 © Time & Life Pictures/Getty Images; p. 37 © Sean Cayton/The Image Works.

Designer: Les Kanturek